D0429638

Looking Through a Telescope

By Linda Bullock

Consultants
David Larwa
National Science Consultant

Nanci R. Vargus, Ed.D.
Assistant Professor of Literacy
University of Indianapolis
Indianapolis, Indiana

Children's Press®
A Division of Scholastic Inc.
New York Toronto London Auckland Sydney
Mexico City New Delhi Hong Kong
Danbury, Connecticut

Designer: Herman Adler Design
Photo Researcher: Caroline Anderson
The photo on the cover shows a boy using a telescope.

Library of Congress Cataloging-in-Publication Data

Bullock, Linda.
  Looking through a telescope / by Linda Bullock.
      p. cm. – (Rookie read-about science)
Includes index.
Summary: Simple text and photographs describe and illustrate how to use
a telescope.
  ISBN 0-516-22873-0 (lib. bdg.)   0-516-27906-8 (pbk.)
  1. Telescope–Juvenile literature. 2. Astronomy–Observers'
manuals–Juvenile literature. [1. Telescopes.] I. Title. II. Series.
  QB88.B85 2003
  522'.2–dc21
                                        2003000514

Hey, Diddle, Diddle.

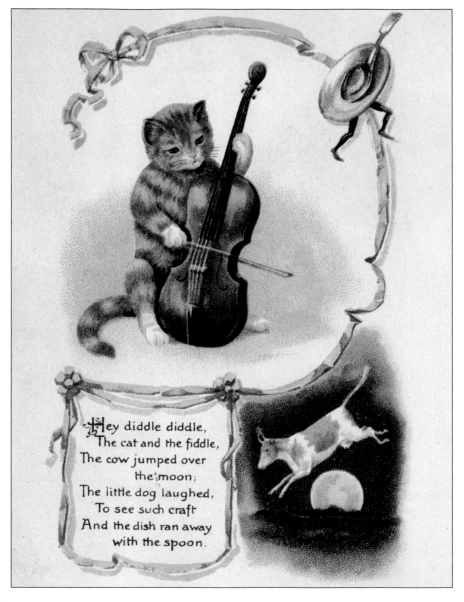

Hey diddle diddle,
The cat and the fiddle,
The cow jumped over
the moon;
The little dog laughed,
To see such craft
And the dish ran away
with the spoon.

4

Did a cow really jump
over the Moon?

Of course not.

Cows eat grass in a field.
Cows sleep in a barn.
Cows cannot jump over
the Moon.

The Moon is a big ball of rock. It is too big to jump over. It is also far away. That is why we cannot see how big it really is.

Look at the Moon.

What does it look like?
Is it bright? Is it shaped
like a ball?

You can use a telescope (TEL-uh-skope) to see what the Moon really looks like.

A telescope is a science tool. It lets us get a closer look at things that are far away.

You can see that the
Moon is big and round
with a telescope.

You can see many craters
on the Moon. Craters
are round holes that are
not deep.

15

16

You can also see maria (MAH-ree-uh) on the Moon. Maria are large areas of dark rock.

Some people say they can see faces in the maria. What do you see?

Telescopes can also help you see planets in space.

Planets are big objects, like Earth, that go around the Sun. Without a telescope, a planet looks like a dot of light in the sky.

Saturn

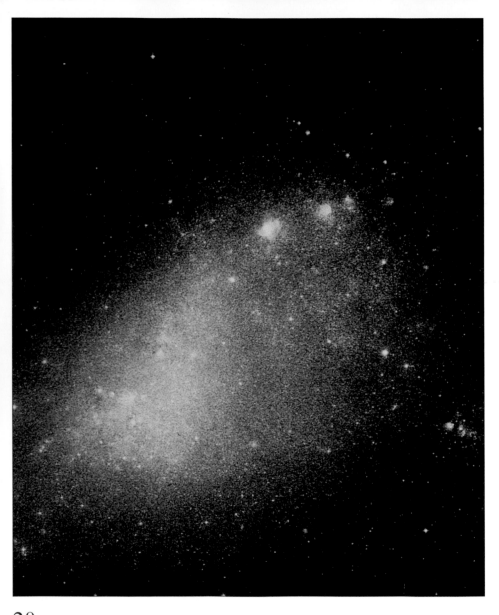

20

You can also use a
telescope to see stars.

Stars are balls of gas.
Some look yellow or
red through a telescope.
Others look blue or white.

Some telescopes are as big as buildings. Scientists use them to see things really far away.

You cannot see some of these things without using a telescope.

23

Scientists have even put
a big telescope into space.
It can see things that
telescopes on Earth cannot.
It is called the Hubble
Space Telescope.

The Hubble Space
Telescope has taken
pictures of big clouds
of gas, dust, and stars.

These pictures help
scientists (SYE-uhn-tists)
learn how stars form.

What do you want to look
at through a telescope?
Will you look at a star?
What about a planet?

Look again.

Words You Know

crater

Hubble Space Telescope

maria

planet

star

telescope

31

Index

About the Author

Dr. Linda Bullock lives in Austin, Texas. So do lots of other people who like to look at the Moon and stars.

Photo Credits